Back to Basics

MATHS

for 9–10 year olds

BOOK TWO

George Rodda

Addition

My buns are fresh!

Cook made...

```
  150 buns on Monday
  252 buns on Tuesday
+  96 buns on Wednesday
  498 buns
```

1 Check that the total of buns is 498.

Work out these additions.

2	3	4	5
443 145 + 201	355 236 + 401	715 105 + 95	427 300 + 293

6	7	8	9
530 203 + 177	215 572 + 98	99 99 + 99	101 98 + 99

10	11	12	13
601 113 + 95	809 72 + 106	721 217 + 172	622 226 + 262

How many buns were made by each baker?

Betty Baker
Mon	120
Tues	132
Wed	96
Thurs	144

_____ buns

Bobbie Baker
Tues	96
Wed	84
Thurs	144
Fri	72

_____ buns

Betsie Baker
Mon	72
Wed	120
Fri	144
Sat	144

_____ buns

Find these totals for Betty, Bobbie and Betsie Baker.

1 Monday buns

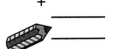
+ _____
_____
_____

2 Tuesday buns

+ _____
_____
_____

3 Wednesday buns

+ _____
_____
_____

4 How many buns were made altogether in the week?

Betty
Bobbie
Betsie   _____
Total   _____ buns

5 Bobbie makes patterns with his buns. Draw the next two patterns for him.

1 bun   4 buns   9 buns   _____ buns   _____ buns

Fill in the missing numbers.

1
```
  8 4
+ 1 ☐
-----
1 0 0
```

2
```
  6 3
+ ☐ 8
-----
  9 1
```

3
```
  5 ☐
+ 4 2
-----
1 0 1
```

4
```
  7 5
+ 1 2 ☐
-------
2 0 0
```

5
```
  ☐ 2 9
  4 0 2
+ 3 4 ☐
-------
  8 7 2
```

6
```
  2 0 ☐
  1 4 7
+ ☐ 1 4
-------
  6 6 2
```

7
```
  5 ☐ 7
    3 ☐
+ 2 4 1
-------
  8 0 1
```

8
```
  2 ☐ 4
  4 2 ☐
+ ☐ 4 2
-------
  9 9 9
```

9 999 added to ☐ makes 1000.

10 500 added to ☐ makes 1000.

Subtraction

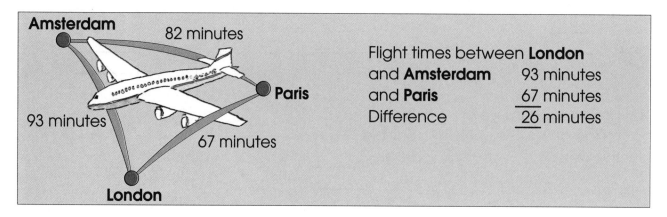

Amsterdam
82 minutes
Paris
93 minutes
67 minutes
London

Flight times between **London**
and **Amsterdam**   93 minutes
and **Paris**   67 minutes
Difference   26 minutes

Check that the difference between 93 and 67 is 26.

93
– 67
_____

93 – 67 = _____

93 minus 67 = _____

Subtract 67 from 93. _____

Work out these flight differences.

1 Between Amsterdam
and London _____ minutes
and Paris _____ minutes
Difference _____ minutes

2 Between Paris
and Amsterdam _____ minutes
and London _____ minutes
Difference _____ minutes

Find these answers.

3 427	**4** 527	**5** 616	**6** 825
– 318	– 418	– 217	– 450
_____	_____	_____	_____

7 1829	**8** 2475	**9** 2736	**10** 2256
– 917	– 283	– 642	– 1047
_____	_____	_____	_____

11 4530	**12** 9111	**13** 8736	**14** 8736
– 1614	– 1911	– 817	– 8017
_____	_____	_____	_____

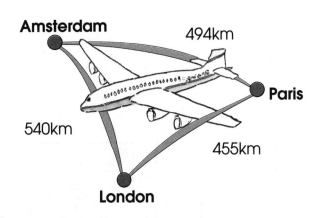

Amsterdam

494km

540km

Paris

455km

London

Find the difference.

1 London to Amsterdam   540 km
              London to Paris _____ km
                    Difference _____ km

2 Paris to Amsterdam _____ km   **3** Amsterdam to London _____ km
        Paris to London _____ km   Amsterdam to Paris _____ km
            Difference _____ km   Difference _____ km

4 Put a tick ✔ by the longer journey.

Paris ⟶ Amsterdam ⟶ London ☐

or   Paris ⟶ London ⟶ Amsterdam ☐

How many km longer is it?   How many minutes longer is it?
            _____ km   _____ minutes

1 Take 99 from 200.   **2** Take 98 from 200.   **3** Take 97 from 200.

_____   _____   _____

4 Take 101 from 200.   **5** Take 102 from 200.   **6** Take 103 from 200.

_____   _____   _____

Fill in the missing numbers.

7 $99 - \boxed{} = 69$ **8** $990 - \boxed{} = 690$

9 $1000 - \boxed{} = 999$ **10** $1000 - \boxed{} = 99$

11   4 7 3   **12**   5 6 4   **13**   4 ☐ 3   **14**   9 8 ☐
       − 2 ☐ 2   − 2 ☐ 5   − 3 8 4   − 8 9 9
       ———————   ———————   ———————   ———————
         2 5 1   3 4 9   1 9   8 1

Mirror lines

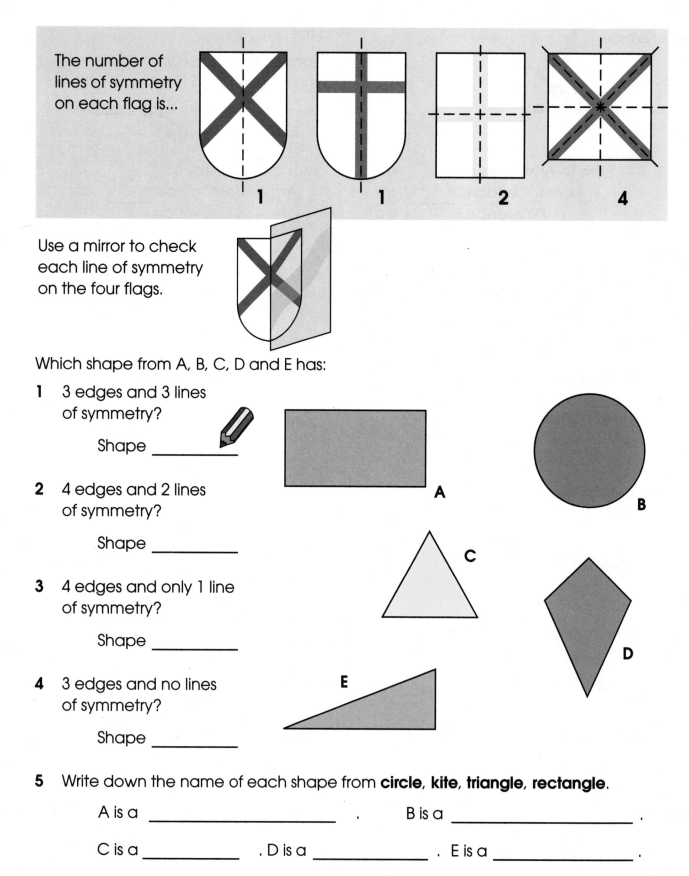

The number of lines of symmetry on each flag is...

1   **1**   **2**   **4**

Use a mirror to check each line of symmetry on the four flags.

Which shape from A, B, C, D and E has:

1   3 edges and 3 lines of symmetry?

Shape _____

2   4 edges and 2 lines of symmetry?

Shape _____

3   4 edges and only 1 line of symmetry?

Shape _____

4   3 edges and no lines of symmetry?

Shape _____

A

B

C

D

E

5   Write down the name of each shape from **circle, kite, triangle, rectangle**.

A is a _____ .   B is a _____ .

C is a _____ . D is a _____ . E is a _____ .

On this rectangle draw:

1 A red line to cut it into 2 squares.

2 A blue line to cut it into 2 triangles.

3 A green line to cut it into 2 rectangles.

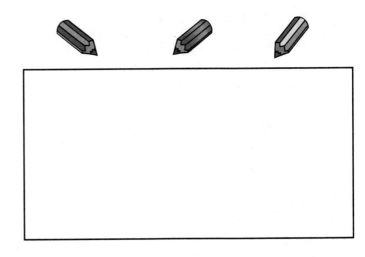

4 The lines drawn are lines of symmetry. Fill in the missing parts of the 3 pictures.

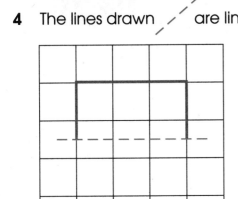 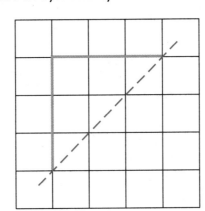 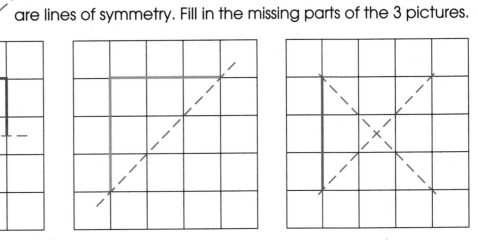

Each finished shape is a _____ .

Draw the lines of symmetry on these pictures.

5

_____ lines

6

_____ lines

7

_____ lines

8

_____ lines

9

_____ lines

10

_____ lines

11

_____ lines

Multiplication

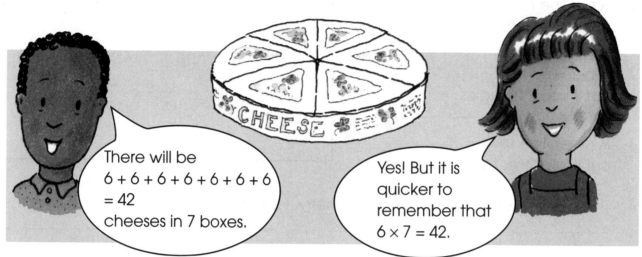

There will be
6 + 6 + 6 + 6 + 6 + 6 + 6
= 42
cheeses in 7 boxes.

Yes! But it is quicker to remember that 6 × 7 = 42.

Work out these sums for boxes of cheese.

1 5 boxes will contain 6 + 6 + 6 + 6 + 6 = _____

or 6 × 5 = _____ cheeses.

2 8 boxes will contain 6 + 6 + 6 + 6 + 6 + 6 + 6 + 6 = _____

or 6 × 8 = _____ cheeses.

Fill in these tables.

3

×	5
1	5
2	
3	
4	
5	
6	30
7	
8	
9	
10	

4

×	6
1	
2	
3	
4	
5	
6	
7	42
8	
9	
10	

5

×	7
1	
2	
3	
4	
5	
6	
7	
8	
9	
10	

6

×	8
1	
2	
3	
4	
5	
6	
7	
8	
9	
10	

Write in the answers.

7 5 × 8 = _____

8 6 × 7 = _____

9 8 × 0 = _____

10 8 × 5 = _____

11 7 × 6 = _____

12 0 × 8 = _____

Finish these multiplications.

1 23 × 2	**2** 23 × 3	**3** 23 × 4	**4** 23 × 5

5 35 × 4	**6** 51 × 8	**7** 42 × 6	**8** 142 × 6

9 213 × 3	**10** 223 × 3	**11** 322 × 5	**12** 405 × 3

13 99 × 9	**14** 499 × 2	**15** 299 × 3	**16** 909 × 2

Work these out.

Edam cheeses are packed 9 in a box.

17 How many cheeses will there be in 7 boxes?

 _____ cheeses

18 How many cheeses will there be in 8 boxes?

_____ cheeses

19 How many cheeses will there be in 10 boxes?

_____ cheeses

Fill in the missing numbers.

20 $7 \times \boxed{} = 56$

21 $9 \times \boxed{} = 0$

22 $\boxed{} \times 10 = 100$

Money

100p = £1

Add up the value of the coins in the picture.

1   1p + 2p + 5p + 10p + 20p + 50p + 100p = _____ p

= £ _____

Fill in the missing numbers.

2   £1   has the same value as [   ] of (1p)

3   £1   has the same value as [   ] of (50p)

4   £1   has the same value as [   ] of (20p)

5   £1   has the same value as [   ] of (10p)

6   £1   has the same value as [   ] of (5p)

7   £1   has the same value as [   ] of (2p)

8   20p   has the same value as [   ] of (5p)

9   50p   has the same value as [   ] of (5p)

How much change do you need?

10   From £1

Spend	85p	45p	99p	2p	39p	72p
Change	p	p	p	p	p	p

11 From £2

Spend	£1.50		40p	£1.90		73p		99p		£1.19
Change	p	£			p	£		£		p

Work out these additions.

1
£
1.25
+ 1.75
£ _____

2
£
2.30
+ 2.70
£ _____

3
£
1.72
+ 1.38
£ _____

4
£
2.75
+ 0.55
£ _____

5
£
4.96
+ 4.96
£ _____

6
£
5.67
+ 3.46
£ _____

7
£
3.85
+ 5.16
£ _____

8
£
1.99
+ 1.99
£ _____

Work out these subtractions.

9
£
4.73
− 1.64
£ _____

10
£
7.56
− 2.67
£ _____

11
£
8.75
− 0.76
£ _____

12
£
10.00
− 1.63
£ _____

Fill in the answers.

1
£1.10
× 6
£ _____

2
£2.25
× 4
£ _____

3
£2.25
× 8
£ _____

4
£3.33
× 6
£ _____

5 £12.50 ÷ 5
= £ _____

6 £11.60 ÷ 4
= £ _____

7 £24.18 ÷ 6
= £ _____

Change these.

1 £2 = _____ p

2 254p = £ _____

3 £2.50 = _____ p

4 309p = £ _____

5 500 p = £ _____

6 25p = £ _____

Solid shapes

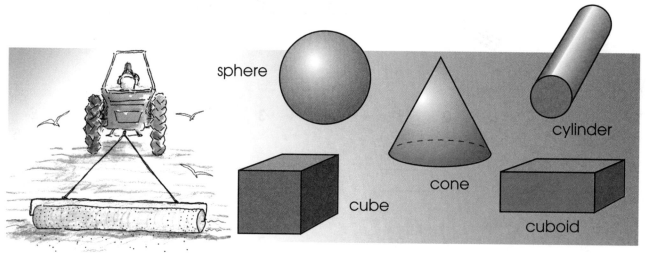

sphere

cone

cylinder

cube

cuboid

1 Write down the name of the solid shape being pulled by the tractor. _____

Name these solids from **sphere, cone, cylinder, cube** and **cuboid**.

2 cube

3  _____

4 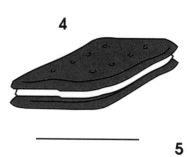 _____

5 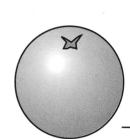 _____

6 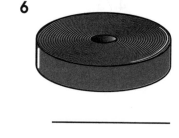 _____

7 Which of the shapes can roll down a slope?

1 _____

2 _____

3 _____

8 Which shape is best for a wheel? _____

9 Which shape makes the best ball? _____

10 Which shape makes the best dice? _____

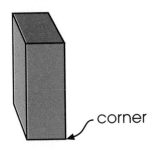

corner

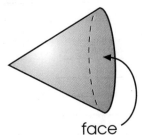

face

Which solid has:

1   faces which are square? _____

2   faces which are rectangles? _____

3   faces which are circles? _____

4   only 1 face which is a circle? _____

5   8 corners? _____

6   only one corner? _____

7   What is the shape of each can of crush? _____

8   What is the shape of the box? _____

← 8 cm →

Each can measures 8cm across.

9   How long is the box? _____ cm

10   How wide is the box? _____ cm

11   Cut out a circle of paper.

Cut to the centre and cut a piece out.

Join the 2 straight cuts at A and B with sticky tape.

You have made a cone!

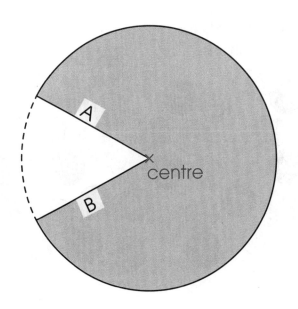

A

× centre

B

Graphs

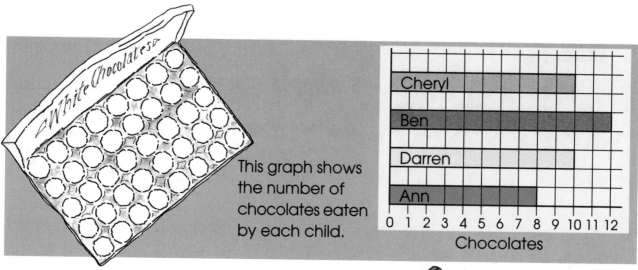

This graph shows the number of chocolates eaten by each child.

1 How many chocolates are there in the box?

2 From the graph, how many will be eaten by:

Ann? ☐   Ben? ☐   Cheryl? ☐   Darren? ☐

Add up your 4 answers.   Total ☐

3 Will there be any chocolates left? _____

On the picture of the box of chocolates colour:
Ann's share red.   Ben's share blue.
Cheryl's share green.   Darren's share yellow.

1 Finish the tally for these buttons.

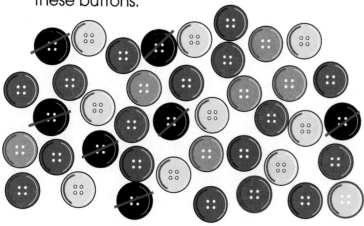

Black	~~||||~~ ||	7
Red		
Blue		
Green		
Yellow		
	Total	40

Check that the total
number of buttons is 40.

Use this grid to draw
a graph showing the
number of buttons of
each colour.

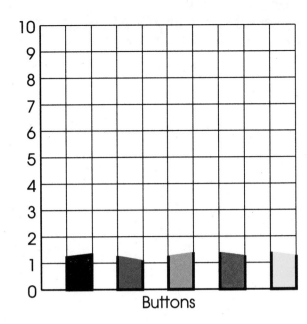

Buttons

Fill in these fractions.

2 $\dfrac{\text{red buttons}}{\text{all the buttons}} = \dfrac{\square}{40} = \dfrac{\square}{4}$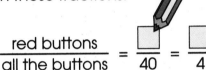

3 $\dfrac{\text{yellow buttons}}{\text{all the buttons}} = \dfrac{\square}{\underline{}}$

4 $\dfrac{\text{red and yellow buttons}}{\text{all the buttons}} = \dfrac{\square}{\underline{}}$

5 $\dfrac{\text{black and blue and green buttons}}{\text{all the buttons}} = \dfrac{\square}{\underline{}}$

Ann has 4 pets.
She has a parrot, a dog, a cat and a rabbit.

This graph shows the
weight of Ann's pets.

From the graph, fill
in these weights.

1 Rabbit ☐ kg

    Dog ☐ kg

    Parrot ☐ kg

    Cat ☐ kg

2 Which is the lightest? _____

3 Which is the heaviest? _____

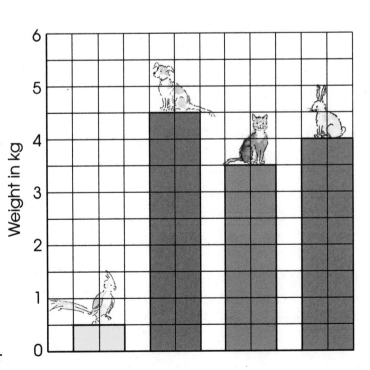

Perimeter

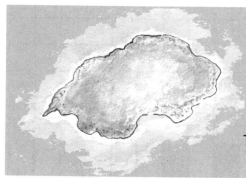

The **perimeter** is the distance round the edge.

The perimeter of this island is 22 kilometres.

1 Fill in the perimeters.

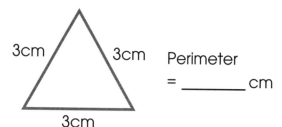

8cm

2cm

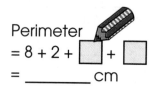

Perimeter
= 8 + 2 + ☐ + ☐
= _____ cm

2

3cm   3cm

3cm

Perimeter
= _____ cm

3

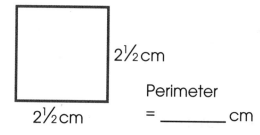

2½cm

2½cm

Perimeter
= _____ cm

On this square grid draw these shapes:

4 A red square with a perimeter of 12cm.

5 A blue rectangle with one edge 2cm long and a perimeter of 12cm.

6 A green rectangle with one edge 1cm long and a perimeter of 12cm.

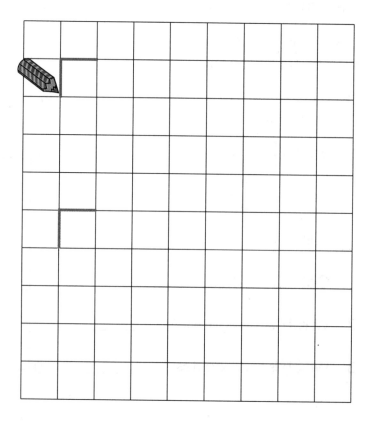

7 Use a piece of string or a strip of paper and a ruler to help you measure these perimeters.

The perimeter of my book is ▢ cm.

The perimeter of my head is ▢ cm.

The perimeter of my plate is ▢ cm.

Use a ruler to measure these perimeters.

1

2

3

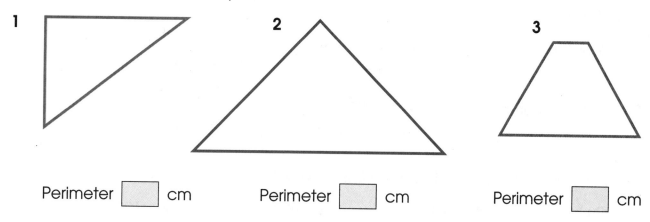

Perimeter ▢ cm   Perimeter ▢ cm   Perimeter ▢ cm

Each of these pencils is 10cm long.
Work out the perimeter of each pattern.

4   **5**   **6**   **7**

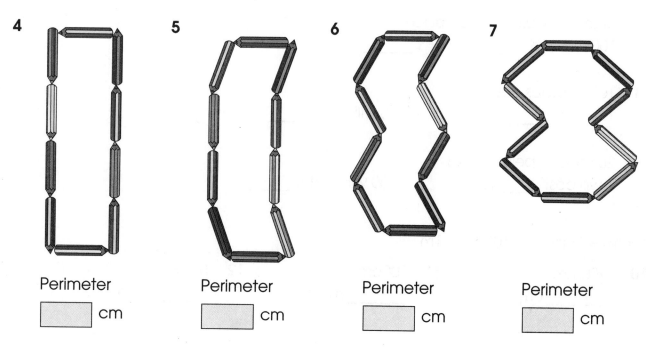

Perimeter
▢ cm

Perimeter
▢ cm

Perimeter
▢ cm

Perimeter
▢ cm

Calculator practice

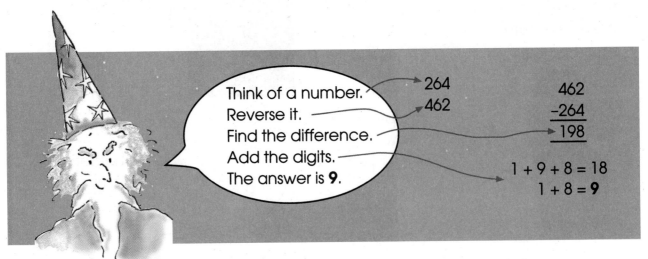

Think of a number. 264
Reverse it. 462
Find the difference.
Add the digits.
The answer is **9**.

462
−264
198

1 + 9 + 8 = 18
1 + 8 = **9**

Check the magician's trick for 264 and make sure that the answer is 9.
Now check these.

1   347 is the number

743 – 347 = 396
3 + 9 + 6 = 18   1 + 8 = [9]

2   994 is the number

994 – 499 = 495
4 + 9 + 5 = 18   1 + 8 = [9]

Use your calculator to show that the trick works with:

3   923   **4**   678   **5**   998   **6**   100

Use your calculator to work these out.

7   Munchie bars cost 80p each.
100 will cost _____ p = £ _____

8   100 Fizzpops cost £9.
1 will cost _____ p   50 will cost £ _____

9   20 magic spells cost £8.
1 will cost _____ p   100 will cost £ _____

10mm = 1cm   100cm = 1m

10   990mm =
_____ cm

11   900cm =
_____ m

12   1m =
_____ mm

These number patterns have been started for you.
Finish the patterns. Check the answers with your calculator.

1

$9 \times 1 - 1 = 8$

$9 \times 21 - 1 = $ _____

$9 \times 321 - 1 = $ _____

$9 \times 4321 - 1 = $ _____

$9 \times 54321 - 1 = $ _____

$9 \times 654321 - 1 = $ _____

2

$9 \times 1 + 2 = 11$

$9 \times 12 + 3 = $ _____

$9 \times 123 + 4 = $ _____

$9 \times 1234 + 5 = $ _____

$9 \times 12345 + 6 = $ _____

$9 \times 123456 + 7 = $ _____

Here is a puzzle for the magician. The signs are missing.

$6 \boxed{} 2 \boxed{} 1 = 11$

Check that the signs are × and –.

$6 \times 2 - 1 = \boxed{}$

Fill in the missing signs from +, –, × and ÷.

1 $6 \boxed{} 2 \boxed{} 1 = 8$

2 $15 \boxed{} 5 \boxed{} 3 = 9$

3 $8 \boxed{} 2 \boxed{} 6 = 10$

4 $12 \boxed{} 12 \boxed{} 2 = 12$

5 $10 \boxed{} 10 \boxed{} 50 = 50$

6 $10 \boxed{} 10 \boxed{} 10 = 10$

Fill in the numbers **2**, **5** or **6**
to make these sums correct.

1 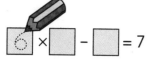 $\boxed{6} \times \boxed{} - \boxed{} = 7$

2 $\boxed{} \times \boxed{} + \boxed{} = 16$

3 $\boxed{} \div \boxed{} + \boxed{} = 8$

4 $\boxed{} \times \boxed{} - \boxed{} = 28$

5 Multiply $1 \times 2 \times 3 \times 4 \times 5 \times 6 \times 7 \times 8 \times 9 = $ _____

Divide and share

3 children can share these 18 balloons.

$18 \div 3$
$= 6$

$3\overline{)18}^{\,6}$

Each can have 6 balloons.

Check the answer by finishing these sums. $3 \times 6 = $  $6 + 6 + 6 = $ ☐

Now answer these.

1 $21 \div 3$
 = _____

2 $18 \div 6$
 = _____

3 $24 \div 2$
 = _____

4 $24 \div 12$
 = _____

5 $27 \div 3$
 = _____

6 $28 \div 7$
 = _____

7 $32 \div 8$
 = _____

8 $24 \div 8$
 = _____

9 $40 \div 10$
 = _____

10 $35 \div 7$
 = _____

11 $55 \div 5$
 = _____

12 $60 \div 5$
 = _____

13 $2\overline{)42}$

14 $3\overline{)33}$

15 $5\overline{)35}$

16 $6\overline{)42}$

17 $3\overline{)45}$

18 $7\overline{)210}$

19 $4\overline{)40}$

20 $4\overline{)400}$

21 If 2 children had shared the 18 balloons, how many could each one have?   ☐ balloons

22 If 6 children had shared the 18 balloons, how many could each one have?   ☐ balloons

23 Colour 4 balloons red, 4 blue, 4 green and 4 yellow.

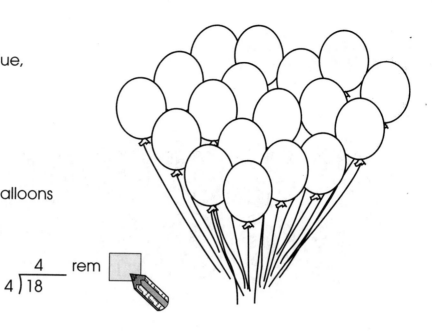

24 If 4 children have 4 balloons each, how many will be left over? [ ] balloons

$$4\overline{)18}\;\dfrac{4}{}\;\text{rem}\;[\;\;]$$

Fill in the answers.

1 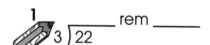 $3\overline{)22}$ _____ rem _____

2 $5\overline{)18}$ _____ rem _____

3 $6\overline{)38}$ _____ rem _____

4 $5\overline{)56}$ _____ rem _____

5 $9\overline{)56}$ _____ rem _____

6 $8\overline{)89}$ _____ rem _____

7 $7\overline{)55}$ _____ rem _____

8 $9\overline{)91}$ _____ rem _____

9 $9\overline{)89}$ _____ rem _____

10 $8\overline{)81}$ _____ rem _____

11 $8\overline{)79}$ _____ rem _____

12 $9\overline{)100}$ _____ rem _____

Find the number of balloons shared out at each party.

1 At a party 4 children have 3 balloons each and there is one remainder.

There were [ ] balloons altogether.

2 At a party 5 children have 3 balloons each and there is one remainder.

There were [ ] balloons altogether.

3 Write two more numbers which have remainder 2 when divided by 4.

2, 6, 10, [ ] , [ ]

Fractions

10p is $\frac{1}{10}$ of £1

$\frac{1}{10} = 0.1$

How many coins make £1? ▢

Fill in this table.

	10p	20p	30p	40p	50p	70p	80p	90p
Fraction of £1	$\frac{1}{10}$	$\frac{2}{10} = \frac{1}{5}$			$\frac{5}{10} = \frac{1}{2}$			
Decimal of £1	0.1	0.2						0.9

Fill in the missing numbers.

1 $\frac{20p}{£1} = \frac{2}{10} = $ 0. 2

2 $\frac{60p}{£1} = \frac{\boxed{}}{10} = \boxed{}$

3 $1 = 2$ halves $= \frac{\boxed{2}}{2}$

4 $1 = 4$ quarters $= \boxed{\dfrac{}{}}$

5 $1 = 10$ tenths $= \boxed{\dfrac{}{}}$

6 $1 = 5$ fifths $= \boxed{\dfrac{}{}}$

7 $\frac{1}{5}$ of £1 $= \boxed{}$ p

8 $\frac{2}{5}$ of £1 $= \boxed{}$ p

9 0.5 of £1 $= \boxed{}$ p

10 0.5 of £2 $= \boxed{}$ p

11 $\frac{1}{4}$ of £1 $= \boxed{}$ p

12 $\frac{1}{4}$ of £4 $= \boxed{}$ p

13 $\frac{1}{2}$ of 80p $= \boxed{}$ p

14 0.5 of 80p $= \boxed{}$ p

A ruler can help you fill in these answers.

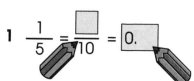

1 $\dfrac{1}{5} = \dfrac{\square}{10} = \boxed{0.\ }$

2 $\dfrac{2}{5} = \dfrac{\square}{10} = \boxed{0.\ }$

3 $\dfrac{4}{5} = \dfrac{\square}{10} = \boxed{0.\ }$

4 Put these in order with the smallest first.

¾, 0.1, ¼, 0.8, 0.6, ½, 0.9

0.1, _____ , _____ , _____ , _____ , _____ , _____

5 This strip of paper has been folded into 10 equal parts.

Fill in these fractions.

Shaded blue $\dfrac{\square}{10} = \boxed{0.\ }$

Shaded red $\dfrac{\square}{10} = \dfrac{\square}{2} = \boxed{0.\ }$

Shaded green $\dfrac{\square}{10} = \dfrac{\square}{5} = \boxed{0.\ }$

6 How many eggs are there in this basket?

Fill in the numbers.

$\dfrac{\square}{5}$ or $\boxed{0.\ }$ are white

$\dfrac{\square}{\square}$ or $\boxed{0.\ }$ are brown

$\dfrac{\square}{\square}$ or $\boxed{0.\ }$ are speckled

Weight

This jockey weighs 56½ kg.

1000 grammes (g) =1 kilogramme (kg)

The jockey's weight is 56½ kg or 56kg ☐ g.

	1	kg	g		2	kg	g		3	kg	g		4	kg	g
		5	500			6	400			3	750			4	750
	+	2	400		+	2	600		+	2	250		+	3	350

	5	kg	g		6	kg	g		7	kg	g		8	kg	g
		6				5	100			3	500			3	600
	-	2	500		-	1	600		-	1	700		-	1	800

	9	kg	g		10	kg	g		11	kg	g		12	kg	g
		1	250			1	500			1	750			4	500
	×		2		×		2		×		2		×		3

13 1kg ÷ 2

= _____ g

14 1kg ÷ 4

= _____ g

15 1kg ÷ 5

= _____ g

16 1kg ÷ 10

= _____ g

17 Add up these weights.

☐ kg ☐ g

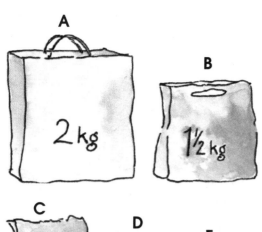

Put the correct letters
A, B, C, D and E
in the answer boxes.

1   Which 2 bags make

    up 1¾ kg?

    ☐ and ☐

2   Which 2 bags make

    up 2½ kg?

    ☐ and ☐   or   ☐ and ☐

3   Which 3 bags make up 3¼ kg?

    ☐ and ☐ and ☐

4   Which 3 bags make up 1¾ kg?

    ☐ and ☐ and ☐

Change these weights to grammes.

1   1kg 500g = _____ g

2   1kg 750g = _____ g

3   2kg 175g = _____ g

4   2kg 75g = _____ g

5   2kg 5g = _____ g

6   2kg 50g = _____ g

Change these weights to kilogrammes and grammes.

1   2500g = _____ kg _____ g

2   2125g = _____ kg _____ g

3   2050g = _____ kg _____ g

4   1005g = _____ kg _____ g

5   10500g = _____ kg _____ g

6   1050g = _____ kg _____ g

Weigh yourself
and write down
your weight.   _____ kg _____ g

Days, hours and minutes

60 minutes = 1 hour
24 hours = 1 day
7 days = 1 week

Write in the minutes on the clock face.

1 How many minutes has the short red hand moved from 12?

2 How many minutes has the long blue hand moved from 12?

```
      0 or 60 mins
mins      12
        11      1
       10          2
mins   9            3    mins
        8          4
          7      5
             6
         mins
```

Fill in the missing numbers.

1 1 hour = [ ] minutes   **2** ½ hour = [ ] minutes

3 ¼ hour = [ ] minutes   **4** ¾ hour = [ ] minutes

Work these out.

1
```
  hr   min
   3    35
+  2    25
_____
```

2
```
  hr   min
   1    40
+  3    40
_____
```

3
```
  hr   min
   5    10
+  2    55
_____
```

4
```
  hr   min
   1    20
×        3
_____
```

5
```
  hr   min
   2    15
×        4
_____
```

6
```
  hr   min
   1    45
×        2
_____
```

Change these to minutes.

7 1hr 15min = _____ min

8 1hr 40min = _____ min

9 1hr 50min = _____ min

10 2hr 20min = _____ min

Fill in the answers.

1 48 hours = _____ days

2 36 hours = _____ days _____ hours

3 40 hours = _____ days _____ hours

The weather should clear in 48 hours.

I can't wait that long...

Work these out.

1
```
 days  hours
   1    12
+  2    12
_____
```

2
```
 days  hours
   2    18
+  3     6
_____
```

3
```
 days  hours
   2    10
+  1    20
_____
```

4
```
 days  hours
   1     0
-        12
_____
```

5
```
 days  hours
   2     6
-        12
_____
```

6
```
 days  hours
   1     9
-        18
_____
```

5 more weeks to the end of term!

Fill in the missing numbers.

1   5 weeks = 5 × _____ days

= _____ days

Only 5 days of the week are school days.

2   5 weeks = _____ school days

3   6 weeks = _____ days

or = _____ school days

4   4 weeks = _____ days

or = _____ school days

5   70 days = 70 ÷ 7 weeks

= _____ weeks

6   73 days

= _____ weeks _____ days

7   1 day = _____ hours = _____ minutes

Capacity

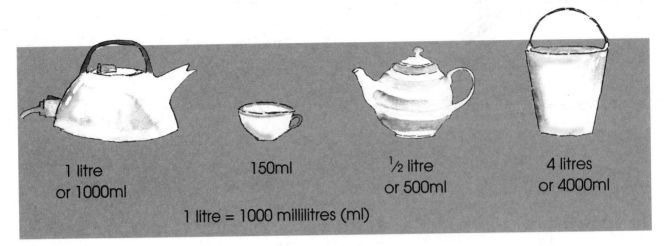

1 litre
or 1000ml

150ml

½ litre
or 500ml

4 litres
or 4000ml

1 litre = 1000 millilitres (ml)

Fill in the answers. Choose from **kettle, cup, teapot** and **bucket**.

1   Which one holds the most?_____

2   Which one holds the least?_____

3   How many times will a full kettle fill the teapot? _____ times

4   How many times will a full bucket fill the kettle? _____ times

5   How many times will a full bucket fill the teapot?_____ times

Work these out.

1	litres	ml
		500
+		600

2	litres	ml
	1	500
+		500

3	litres	ml
	1	500
+	1	750

4	litres	ml
	2	750
+	1	300

5	litres	ml
	2	350
+	2	750

6	litres	ml
	1	75
+	1	75

7   1 cupful and 1 teapot full will hold _____ millilitres.

8	litres	ml
	2	500
−	1	400

9	litres	ml
	1	
−		500

10	litres	ml
	1	
−		600

11	litres	ml
	2	500
−	1	700

12	litres	ml
	3	50
−	1	100

13	litres	ml
	4	10
−	2	100

14	litres	ml
	1	250
×		4

15	litres	ml
	2	200
×		6

16	litres	ml
	5	400
×		3

Change these millilitres to litres and millilitres.

1 1050ml

= _____ litres _____ ml

2 1500ml

= _____ litres _____ ml

3 2005ml

= _____ litres _____ ml

4 1001ml

= _____ litres _____ ml

Write in the answers.

1 1 litre ÷ 2

= _____ ml

2 1 litre ÷ 4

= _____ ml

3 1 litre ÷ 10

= _____ ml

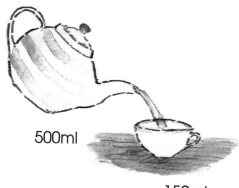

500ml

150ml

4 How many times can you fill the cup from the teapot?

_____ times

How many millilitres will be left in the pot?

_____ millilitres left

Metres, centimetres and millimetres

10 millimetres = 1 centimetre
(mm)   (cm)

100 centimetres = 1 metre
(cm)   (m)

Robin's arrows are too short.
He needs them to be 80cm long.

1 Measure this arrow in centimetres.

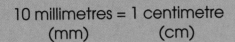 cm

Now measure it in millimetres. mm

Robin's arrows need to be 80cm long.

2 These arrows are too short for him.

Length of arrow	70cm	79cm	68cm	68½cm	79½cm
Short by	10cm	cm	cm	cm	cm

3

Length of arrow	79½cm	79cm	75cm	70cm	69½cm
Short by	mm	mm	mm	mm	mm

4 These arrows are too long for Robin.

Length of arrow	1m	90cm	1m 10cm	95cm	1½m
Too long by	20cm	cm	cm	cm	cm

Work these out

1
```
  cm  mm
   4   5
+  2   5
───────
```

2
```
  cm  mm
   3   7
+  4   6
───────
```

3
```
  cm  mm
   5   4
+  3   9
───────
```

4
```
  cm  mm
   4   9
+  3   9
───────
```

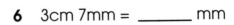

5 2cm 5mm = _____ mm

6 3cm 7mm = _____ mm

7 42mm = _____ cm _____ mm   **8** 51mm = _____ cm _____ mm

9
```
    m   cm
    2   60
+   3   40
_____
```

10
```
    m   cm
    3   75
+   2   30
_____
```

11
```
    m   cm
    4   49
+   3   52
_____
```

12 1m 25cm = _____cm   **13** 2m 5cm = _____cm

14 350cm = _____ m _____cm   **15** 207cm = _____ m_____cm

Fill in the missing numbers for these arrows.

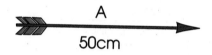
A
50cm

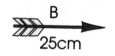
B
25cm

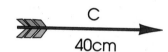
C
40cm

End to end

1 _____ of arrow A measures 1 metre.

2 _____ of arrow B measures 1 metre.

3 _____ of arrow C measures 2 metres.

4 3 of arrow A + 2 of arrow B measure _____ metres.

5 3 of arrow B + 2 of arrow C measure _____ cm

             or _____ m _____ cm

Work these out.

1
```
  cm   mm
  10   5
-  1   6
_____
```

2
```
   m   cm
   3   50
-  1   51
_____
```

3
```
   m   cm
   4   49
-  2   50
_____
```

4

Use a tape measure or piece of string
to find the length of this arrow.

_____ cm

Answers

To Parents: We have not provided *all* the answers here. We suggest that items to be coloured in on squares. lengths and graphs should be checked by you. In the case of activities where calculations are performed by your child, it would be good practice to get him/her to use a calculator to check the answers.

Page 2

2 789 **3** 992 **4** 915 **5** 1020
6 910 **7** 885 **8** 297 **9** 298
10 809 **11** 987 **12** 1110 **13** 1110
Betty 492 Bobbie 396 Betsie 480

Page 3

1 192 **2** 228 **3** 300 **4** 1368
5 16; 25
1 6 **2** 2 **3** 9 **4** 5
5 1; 1 **6** 1; 3 **7** 2; 3 **8** 3; 3; 3
9 1 **10** 500

Page 4

1 11 **2** 15 **3** 109 **4** 109
5 399 **6** 375 **7** 912 **8** 2192
9 2094 **10** 1209 **11** 2916 **12** 7200
13 7919 **14** 719

Page 5

1 85 **2** 39 **3** 46
4 Paris → Amsterdam → London;
39km; 15min
1 101 **2** 102 **3** 103 **4** 99 **5** 98
6 97 **7** 30 **8** 300 **9** 1 **10** 901
11 2 **12** 1 **13** 0 **14** 0

Page 6

1 C **2** A **3** D **4** E **5** A rectangle;
B circle; C triangle; D kite; E triangle

Page 7

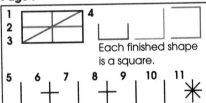

Each finished shape is a square.

Page 8

1 30 **2** 48
3 10,15, 20, 25, 35, 40, 45, 50
4 6, 12, 18, 24, 30, 36, 48, 54, 60
5 7, 14, 21, 28, 35, 42, 49, 56, 63, 70
6 8, 16, 24, 32, 40, 48, 56, 64, 72, 80
7 40 **8** 42 **9** 0 **10** 40
11 42 **12** 0

Page 9

1 46 **2** 69 **3** 92 **4** 115
5 140 **6** 408 **7** 252 **8** 852
9 639 **10** 669 **11** 1610 **12** 1215
13 891 **14** 998 **15** 897 **16** 1818
17 63 **18** 72 **19** 90 **20** 8
21 0 **22** 10

Page 10

1 188; 1.88 **2** 100 **3** 2
4 5 **5** 10 **6** 20 **7** 50
8 4 **9** 10 **10** 15, 55, 1, 98, 61, 28

Page 11

11 50, 1.60, 10, 1.27, 1.01, 81
1 3.00 **2** 5.00 **3** 3.10 **4** 3.30
5 9.92 **6** 9.13 **7** 9.01 **8** 3.98
9 3.09 **10** 4.89 **11** 7.99 **12** 8.37
1 6.60 **2** 9.00 **3** 18.00 **4** 19.98
5 2.50 **6** 2.90 **7** 4.03
1 200 **2** 2.54 **3** 250 **4** 3.09
5 5 **6** 0.25

Page 12

1 cylinder **2** cube **3** cone
4 cuboid **5** sphere **6** cylinder
7 sphere; cylinder; cone - but not in a straight line **8** cylinder **9** sphere
10 cube

Page 13

1 cube **2** cuboid **3** cylinder
4 cone **5** cube or cuboid
6 cone **7** cylinder **8** cuboid
9 24 **10** 16

Page 14

1 40 **2** 8; 12; 10; 10; Total 40 **3** No
1 R10; B7; G6; Y10

Page 15

2 10; 1 **3** ¼ **4** ½ **5** ½
1 R4; D4½; P½; C3½ **2** Parrot **3** Dog

Page 16

1 20 **2** 9 **3** 10 **4** 3 by 3
5 2 by 4 **6** 1 by 5

Page 17

1 12 **2** 17 **3** 11 **4** 100
5 100 **6** 100 **7** 100

Page 18

7 8000; 80 **8** 9; 4.50 **9** 40; 40
10 99 **11** 9 **12** 1000

Page 19

1 188 **2** 111 **1** +, ÷ **2** ÷, x
   2888   1111 **3** ÷, + or x, – **4** +, ÷
   38888   11111 **5** ÷, x or –, +
   488888 111111 **6** x, ÷ or ÷, x
   5888888 1111111   or –, +, or +, –
1 6, 2, 5 **2** 2, 5, 6 or 5, 2, 6
3 6, 2, 5 **4** 6, 5, 2 or 5, 6, 2
5 362880

Page 20

1 7 **2** 3 **3** 12 **4** 2
5 9 **6** 4 **7** 4 **8** 3
9 4 **10** 5 **11** 11 **12** 12
13 21 **14** 11 **15** 7 **16** 7
17 15 **18** 30 **19** 10 **20** 100
21 9 **22** 3

Page 21

24 2; 4 rem 2
1 7 rem 1 **2** 3 rem 3 **3** 6 rem 2
4 11 rem 1 **5** 6 rem 2 **6** 11 rem 1
7 7 rem 6 **8** 10 rem 1 **9** 9 rem 8
10 10 rem 1 **11** 9 rem 7 **12** 11 rem 1
1 13 **2** 16 **3** 14, 18

Page 22

		³/₁₀	⁴/₁₀ = ²/₅		⁷/₁₀	⁸/₁₀ = ⁴/₅	⁹/₁₀
		0.3	0.4	0.5	0.7	0.8	

1 0.2 **2** 0.6 **3** ²/₂ **4** ⁴/₄
5 ¹⁰/₁₀ **6** ⁵/₅ **7** 20 **8** 40
9 50 **10** 100 **11** 25 **12** 100
13 40 **14** 40

Page 23

1 ²/₁₀, 0.2 **2** ⁴/₁₀, 0.4 **3** ⁸/₁₀, 0.8
4 ¼, ½, 0.6, ¾, 0.8, 0.9
5 B ³/₁₀, 0.3, R ⁵/₁₀, ½, 0.5, G ²/₁₀, ⅕, 0.2
6 W ⅕, 0.2, B ²/₅, 0.4, Sp ²/₅, 0.4

Page 24

1 7kg 900g **2** 9kg **3** 6kg
4 8kg 100g **5** 3kg 500g **6** 3kg 500g
7 1kg 800g **8** 1kg 800g **9** 2kg 500g
10 3kg **11** 3kg 500g **12** 13kg 500g
13 500 **14** 250 **15** 200
16 100 **17** 2kg 250g

Page 25

1 B and E **2** A and D or B and C
3 A and C and E **4** C and D and E
1 1500 **2** 1750 **3** 2175
4 2075 **5** 2005 **6** 2050
1 2kg 500g **2** 2kg 125g **3** 2kg 50g
4 1kg 5g **5** 10kg 500g **6** 1kg 50g

Page 26

1 24 **2** 53
1 60 **2** 30 **3** 15 **4** 45
1 6hr **2** 5hr 20min **3** 8hr 5min
4 4hr **5** 9hr **6** 3 hr 30min
7 75 **8** 100 **9** 110 **10** 140

Page 27

1 2 **2** 1 day 12hr **3** 1 day 16hr
1 4 days **2** 6 days **3** 4 days 6hr
4 12hr **5** 1 day 18hr **6** 15hr
1 7,35 **2** 25 **3** 42 or 30
4 28 or 20 **5** 10 weeks
6 10 weeks 3 days **7** 24, 1440

Page 28

1 bucket **2** cup **3** 2 **4** 4 **5** 8
1 1l 100ml **2** 2l **3** 3l 250ml
4 4l 50ml **5** 5l 100ml **6** 2l 150ml
7 650ml